Chelle Calling! (life as a zebra)

Journal of an Ehlers Danlos Syndrome Sufferer

Chelle Calling!
(life as a zebra)

The premise of this story was to give an insight into a life lived with an inherent/genetic condition.

I dedicate this book to the three most important people in my life:

My three Muses

My three Furies

Triple lock upon my heart

GORDON, SINEAD, ARYA

A Journal from an Ehlers
Danlos Syndrome Sufferer

Chelle Calling!
(life as a zebra)

A Journal from an Ehlers
Danlos Syndrome Sufferer

Chelle Calling!
(life as a zebra)

A Journal from an Ehlers
Danlos Syndrome Sufferer

Chelle Calling!
(life as a zebra)

DAY 1

Hi I'm Chelle, I'm 53 years old, and have recently been diagnosed with (h)EDS. Note the thought that if I had been brave enough or even remotely technologically savvy, this would have been a trendy speech bubble in a sound bite, pod cast, call it whatever!! Alas the Luddite in me, archaic paper and ink will need to suffice. This is the woman who went into complete meltdown, when her husband broached the subject of a new mobile phone. Talk about having the horrors!! I was practically having a full-blown tantrum. I do not cope with change or tech very well. It was at least a week before I could even have a look at the new phone, and then realising it didn't have the same size of sim card, was enough to tip me over the edge. We ended up going into the Apple store in Glasgow for some assistance.

However back to today, the next trendy thought would have been to display written placards a la Dylan, dylanesque (is that a word?????)., Mr Bob Dylan (love his song writing and his songs being sung by other people, but I'm afraid not Bob himself, sorry Bob) Three words, three placards, each word stark and bold (h)EHLERS DANLOS

A Journal from an Ehlers
Danlos Syndrome Sufferer

Chelle Calling!
(life as a zebra)

SYNDROME. The lower-case letter h, stands for hypermobility, I would say directly to camera.

Now I know I'm ahead of myself, again. The initial concept had been short, snappy sound bites, maximum of fifteen minutes of concentration for the reader, allowing for cerebral cognitive processes to operate as expected. You will have heard people talk about fibromyalgia (fibro fog), brain fog, automation functions only. Where despite your best efforts, the neuro transmitters have misfired yet again, generally when you least need or want them to. In short, the term is simply a "brain fart". That massive internal central processing unit is on strike and you may as well be tingling a triangle in a vaulted cathedral!! It's not a lack of intelligence or a pre disposition to early on set dementia. It's the neurological unit taking a Staycation!! Yip, lights are on!!

See, digression!! What is Ehlers Danlos Syndrome? Before I take this very intrusive condition and try to serve it as a single cell amoeba, please believe me, it is far from that. It's a multi tentacled entity, which leeches mercilessly throughout your body's system, Octopus, Octopi!!

I'm not here to take issues with or debunk any clinical research and lengthy physiological and anatomical studies, that have taken place over centuries, yes centuries, but merely to provide an insight to adverse experiences I

A Journal from an Ehlers
Danlos Syndrome Sufferer

Chelle Calling!
(life as a zebra)

encountered and merely my thought process and observations. I am by no means a professional on the human species, only a traveller on life's journey, letting you the reader, see my life through a lens, if you will.

So in most raw terms Ehlers Danlos Syndrome is technically categorised as a Musco skeletal condition. There are over 13 different types, don't worry, we don't need to research them individually. I would just like you to come with me for a little while. Some days it may get a bit messy, a bit technical, but it won't be like that every day, I promise.

For those of you who have persevered to this point, thank you so much. To those of you who have or are about to give up and think "Whoah!!" way too much "heavy" for me here. That's also OK, again thank you for what you did manage to read, before choosing this isn't for you, I get it, I really do.

I'm for a rest now anyway, but before I do a disease described by Hippocrates as far back as 400 BC, matches many of the triggers, responses, signs, symptoms of Ehlers Danlos Syndrome.

A Journal from an Ehlers
Danlos Syndrome Sufferer

Chelle Calling!
(life as a zebra)

PS: Forgot to say I live in Argyll and Bute on the West Coast of Scotland, the only place where it rains sideways!!

A Journal from an Ehlers
Danlos Syndrome Sufferer

Chelle Calling!
(life as a zebra)

DAY 2

Good evening, Dear reader, from this Strange Little Girl (shout out to the family in black), The Stranglers fans, Dave Greenfield.........musical legend, RIP and more recently Jet Black, RIP.

And straight off, I'm not where I wanted to be. Todays' entry was designed more by way of apology for the first entry!! I don't want this journal to become a self-indulgent, self-denigrating diatribe. A staccato narration of despair and forelock tugging.

Ehlers Danlos (EDS) is a genetically inherent condition. Is that a double adjective?

A Journal from an Ehlers
Danlos Syndrome Sufferer

Chelle Calling!
(life as a zebra)

There are many people in the world living a perfectly ordinary life, doing ordinary things, who are unaware that they may carry this "sleekit" DNA coding.

Unfortunately for those of us, who seem to manifest the myriad symptoms, ailments masquerading as other more commonly diagnosed medical conditions, it is an imperfect puzzle, that we may never be given all the pieces to.

Only by medical research and those with diagnosed EDS sharing their lived experiences, will we ever move forward in the search for the missing pieces.

Think about your own immediate inner circle, you will know someone who has been told by their GP, it's CFS, ME, CVS, fibromyalgia, your gastric issues, "Ah well". The aforementioned diseases can go hand in glove: IBS, Crohn's disease, acid reflux.

What if, somehow their genetic coding could be collated, tested, recorded and prove genetic lineage, maybe a medication could be invented. A drug that really did help

A Journal from an Ehlers
Danlos Syndrome Sufferer

EDS sufferers maintain a healthier, pain free, more positive lifestyle. Researchers have currently been unable to isolate the mutated gene.

No more pregabalin, naproxen, anti-depressants, etc.

Chelle Calling!
(life as a zebra)

Day 3

I'm currently convalescing at home, now, there is a quaint old statement!! Convalescing, by the sea, (Kyles of Bute) lots of lovely fresh air. How very Victorian!!

I'm well aware that I'm off kilter, my axis has slipped, away with the fairies, endless descriptions, but you get the picture.

I had not suffered a bout of Cyclical vomiting (CVS) for well over ten years, so in actual fact, damn well under control, or so I thought. CVS is, by the way, another one of those tentacles I was talking about.

A Journal from an Ehlers
Danlos Syndrome Sufferer

Chelle Calling!
(life as a zebra)

Saturday night: 5th November, Bonfire night, fireworks!! Don't worry I won't ignite that debate, except to say I can see both points of view. That aside my granddaughter is merely 7 years old, she wins every time, fireworks it is.

My daughter and granddaughter still live in Ayrshire, so off down the A78 we excitedly drove, full of plans. Get the butcher in Saltcoats for the most amazing black pudding. Kandy Bar pies!! (Shameless plug, they have to be tried!!). Aldi for a reserve box of fireworks, the one we had with us had been residing on a shelf in the kitchen for around 2 years.

It was a pretty wild, windy old day, by the time we reached Saltcoats. Fireworks purchased, Kandy Bar and butchers sorted, we headed to our daughters' home.

We had a fantastic time, especially the little one and myself (Nana), give us both sparklers, works every time!! Most of the houses round about must have had the same idea, so it was lovely to see the other displays lighting the skies. The weather had dramatically improved.

A Journal from an Ehlers
Danlos Syndrome Sufferer

Chelle Calling!
(life as a zebra)

Later, we adults, being horror buffs snuggled down for an evening of chasing that initial buzz of fear, the attempt to recreate that first jolt, the shock, excitement, heart beat racing nano second of original fear. I think we have become increasingly desensitised over the years as we become more accustomed to viewing and possibly accepting of violence in film.

Sunday morning, the plan was to be up, washed, dressed, coffee, breakfast and get ourselves moving. Try Aldi on the way home for more fireworks (planning in advance), compost for the garden.

Sunday morning, actual events, up, washed, dressed, coffee. Hmmm, don't feel 100%, not liking this coffee. Classic indicator number one. I thought OK, leave the coffee, the nauseous feeling will pass. I'll go to the local shop and buy hot filled rolls for breakfast, maybe I just need fresh air.

On the way back from the shop, I felt sluggish and not really that centrally focussed, does that make sense? I was also experiencing a hot flush, more on that later.

A Journal from an Ehlers
Danlos Syndrome Sufferer

Chelle Calling!
(life as a zebra)

Got into the house, put the packages of food on the living room table, saw a lovely fresh coffee, sat on my coaster, took my jacket off, turned to thank my daughter for the coffee and sat down.

All set for my hot roll, took one bite, panicked, stared at my husband like a mad thing, then ran to the upstairs toilet, vomited my first coffee and the rollercoaster nightmare began.

I cleaned myself up, and came back downstairs, perched on the couch. My husband asked if I was alright. I could feel the colour leaching from my skin, that sudden watery mouth feeling, the excess saliva, that represents the upcoming tide. I was about to say no, when the dumph, dumph, dumph of that little telling pulse, that signifies a CVS bout kicked in. The pulse is consistent in its placement, approximately 1-inch to the left of my belly button. Classic indicator number two.

At this point if I was unsure if this was a momentary bout or a full-blown episode, this was pretty much CVS 101: It's happening! So maybe a wee sleep, just for a couple of hours, things will be OK, we do need to get home. I've got work in the morning, my daughter has work, the wee one has school. Nothing improved in that two-hour period. I had now sweated profusely all over my daughters' bed and had no energy to change the bed sheets for her.

A Journal from an Ehlers
Danlos Syndrome Sufferer

Chelle Calling!
(life as a zebra)

I realise this is nose diving fast into a woe is me tale. I think, maybe I will find my Facebook post about this, and just drop it in here.

First night home from hospital, , post dehydration, post delusionary state and a hefty dose of prescription medication I thought , brilliant my own bed again and surely still feeling really quite weak and wobbly, I would have no problem getting a good night sleep. How wrong was I? Prescription medications wearing off, the lack of my normal regulated medication for several days, delusion gradually fading and the rehydration process commencing, I felt as though I saw every hour until around 7am, damn the natural world waking up is noisy!!

Meanwhile I'm popping a little poem in here, whilst I curl up in a ball somewhere and listen to Julian Cope singing about mushroom tea making him all of a quiver.

6am

Tentative tweet of a morning chorus due

The sigh of silver fairy bells

Snip, snip, snip the beetles gleefully munch the dawn fresh grass

Echo of a sea shanty twirling on the breeze

Twelve wailing pipers stomping with leaden feet

Cacophony in my head

A Journal from an Ehlers
Danlos Syndrome Sufferer

Chelle Calling!
(life as a zebra)

It's 6am, the worlds' abed

x

A Journal from an Ehlers
Danlos Syndrome Sufferer

Chelle Calling!
(life as a zebra)

Day 4

Todays' plan is to be more methodical.

I'll give you some of the symptoms that can occur with an EDS sufferer.

I'll try and stay on track, I'm like a seven-legged spider, weaving an imperfect web, no matter how many silken threads are spun, that eighth leg is needed to square the circle.

The paragraphs below are direct from NHS inform and other helpful websites

Hypermobility syndrome symptoms
The main presenting features are joint hypermobility with exercise-related muscle and joint pains and some level of fatigue. However, there is enormous variability in symptom severity. Commonly the history is of:

A Journal from an Ehlers
Danlos Syndrome Sufferer

Chelle Calling!
(life as a zebra)

- Joint/muscle pains after activity and at night - usually lower-limb than upper- limb - most typically, calf and thigh muscles and knees. Younger children tend to report more pain, possibly because teenagers are developing stronger, tighter muscles.
- Swelling, heat or redness are not usually present, unless there is associated injury.
- Muscle and joint stiffness occur the day after activity, often for several days.
- Fatigue, often with reduced exercise tolerance. This relates to deconditioning through exercise avoidance and may impact on all aspects of life, affecting energy levels and concentration.
- Fidgetiness, probably from deconditioned muscles.
- Headaches, often relating to trapezius muscle spasm and poor sitting posture.
- Easy bruising.
- Clicking of joints, both spontaneously and deliberately. Clicking the joints will not harm them unless it becomes obsessive.
- Reduced co-ordination and balance, probably secondary to reduced core strength, leading to clumsiness.

A Journal from an Ehlers
Danlos Syndrome Sufferer

Chelle Calling!
(life as a zebra)

- Handwriting may fatigue easily and fine motor control may be affected.
- A small proportion may have problems with abdominal pain with or without bladder and bowel dysfunction. It is not always clear whether this relates directly. Abdominal pain is common in childhood and frequently relates to constipation. Constipation may increase in incidence when there is reduction in physical activity and muscle tone.
- Rare associations are:
  - Postural orthostatic tachycardia syndrome (PoTS).
  - Hernia: studies of children with hernia have shown that they show an increased prevalence of Beighton score of 4 or more compared to the general population[5].
  - Uterine or rectal prolapse.
  - Joint dislocation (although subluxation is slightly more common).

- A 2005 review of a UK population of 125 children diagnosed with benign joint hypermobility syndrome (BJHS) found that[6]:

  - Average age at onset of symptoms was 6.2 years and age at diagnosis 9.0 years.

A Journal from an Ehlers Danlos Syndrome Sufferer

Chelle Calling!
(life as a zebra)

- The major presenting complaint was arthralgia in 74%, abnormal gait in 10%, apparent joint deformity in 10% and back pain in 6%.
- Mean age at first walking was 15.0 months; 48% were considered 'clumsy' and 36% as having poor co-ordination in early childhood.
- 12% had 'clicky' hips at birth and 4% actual congenital dislocatable hip.
- Urinary tract infections were present in 13% and 6% of the female and male cases, respectively. 14% had speech and learning difficulties diagnosed.
- History of recurrent joint sprains was seen in 20%.
- Actual subluxation/dislocation of joints was seen in 10%.
- 40% had problems with handwriting tasks.
- 48% had major limitations of school-based physical education activities.
- 67% had major limitations of other physical activities.
- 41% had missed significant periods of schooling because of symptoms.
- 43% described easy bruising.
- 94% scored > or =4/9 on the Beighton scale for generalised hypermobility, with knees

A Journal from an Ehlers
Danlos Syndrome Sufferer

(92%), elbows (87%), wrists (82%), hand metacarpophalangeal joints (79%) and ankles (75%) being most frequently involved.

Diagnosis[7]
Diagnosis is clinical, using the widely accepted Brighton criteria. These combine the Beighton hypermobility score (first developed to quantify joint laxity in Ehlers-Danlos syndrome) with symptoms. There are no confirming genetic or biochemical tests.

Beighton hypermobility score[8]
The Beighton hypermobility score is a 9-point scoring system to quantify joint laxity and hypermobility. A higher score equates to higher joint laxity. The threshold for joint laxity in a young adult is 4-6, with scores above 4 correlating well with pain levels in patients diagnosed with benign joint hypermobility syndrome.

Hypermobile Ehlers-Danlos syndrome
This is the most common form of EDS. It is inherited but so far no gene has been identified as the cause. It can be mild and is probably often undiagnosed. However many

Chelle Calling!
(life as a zebra)

people with hEDS have significant or even severe pain and disability.

The main symptoms of hEDS are stretchy skin (which is not fragile but which may heal slowly) and unusually flexible joints.

Many people with hEDS have tiredness, pain and mood changes. The symptoms may include include:

- Sleep disturbance and tiredness.
- Fast heart rate.
- Dizziness and fainting on standing up quickly.
- Unexplained tummy pains, constipation and irritable bowel syndrome.
- Tendency to nausea.
- Anxiety and depression and panic attacks.
- Problems with passing urine.
- Widespread pain in the muscles and/or limbs.
- Headaches.
- Prolapse affecting the bladder, womb (uterus) or back passage.

As you can see there are a vast number of symptoms, some of which I have, others I really hope I don't.

What isn't mentioned in these web sites is dentistry. Many EDS clients have microdontia (small peg shaped teeth),

A Journal from an Ehlers
Danlos Syndrome Sufferer

Chelle Calling!
(life as a zebra)

problems with their TMJ (Tempero mandibular joint) either by having a constant clicking from the jaw joint, or pain/difficulty on opening. They may also be more prone to calculus build up, despite rigorous brushing regimes.

Another strange tentacle is poor night vision. I know that headlights have become increasingly brighter over the years, but night time driving is pretty scary for me. The long winter nights and dark mornings are particularly worrying. I can be blinded by both oncoming lights and the lights of the car behind. I remain dazzled for several seconds afterward.

I remember coming back from covering a clinic in Lochgilphead and a car came racing up behind me, it felt as though they were on full beam, they then proceeded to tailgate me. I could not see anything, and was ultimately down to a crawl in the hope that they would overtake, but they just kept tailgating. I eventually had to indicate and pull into a layby. I was absolutely terrified, I genuinely could see nothing in front of me, the glare of the lights seared my eyeballs!!

Two very good sites for those with EDS, are EDS Scotland and EDS UK. They are both forums which enable us to discuss, share and hopefully support other zebras out there.

A Journal from an Ehlers
Danlos Syndrome Sufferer

Chelle Calling!
(life as a zebra)

Why the Zebra?

"When you hear the sound of hooves, think horses, not zebras."

This phrase is taught to medical students throughout their training.

In medicine, the term "zebra" is used in reference to a rare disease or condition. Doctors are taught to assume that the simplest explanation is usually correct to avoid patients being misdiagnosed with rare illnesses. Doctors learn to expect common conditions.

But many medical professionals seem to forget that "zebras" DO exist and so getting a diagnosis and treatment can be more difficult for sufferers of rare conditions. Ehlers-Danlos syndrome is considered a rare condition and so EDS sufferers are known as medical zebras. This identity has now been adopted across the world through social media to help bring our community together.

A Journal from an Ehlers
Danlos Syndrome Sufferer

Chelle Calling!
(life as a zebra)

A Journal from an Ehlers
Danlos Syndrome Sufferer

Chelle Calling!
(life as a zebra)

Day 5

Time for a wee bit of background.

I was born to mixed race parents, by that I mean a Scots father and a half English/Welsh mother.

I identify as Scots

My father was apparently quite disgusted as his plan was to be North of the Border in time for my arrival. I guess my appearance 17 days early caused the slip up on which side of the border my birth would be documented.

I was apparently a very sickly baby, wouldn't keep anything down. I only now know that was the harbinger of CVS, a symptom of EDS, no-one picked up on.

I have the most amazing GP now, who just happens to be Ade Edmonsons' doppelganger.

He has patiently sat with me and gone through my childhood records and it's all there, the vomiting, the recurrent UTIs, concern about me turning one of my feet in.

A Journal from an Ehlers
Danlos Syndrome Sufferer

Chelle Calling!
(life as a zebra)

It also details, unfortunately the family issues. My parents weren't happy and this pervaded the semblance and structure of family life for me. I was aware of the difficulties between them and it seemed, (to me) that I was the root cause. I was the scapegoat, they yelled at each other, they yelled at me. There is also a social work report, saying that the parents were shouting at each other and that my father had resorted to name calling, as well as shouting at me. This sadly kind of breaks a four-year-old child.

I now understand that my mother, or the biological, which I call her, had lots of issues. Possibly post-natal depression amongst others, which would have done nothing to assist the situation. If she ever got professional help as suggested I will never know. I only hope she did,

I had just completed my British Amateur Gymnastics Awards (BAGA), level 4 and level 3, and had started working toward level 2, another obvious sign, super flexible, super bendy. You would always find me swinging from gates, monkey bars, climbing frames, or tumbling cartwheels, which I loved to do and probably still could do them up until my late 40s. I dare not try it now. When the decision to move was made.

We moved in 1974 from the Lake District to Glenbranter a forestry village in Argyll. It should have been heaven. It wasn't.

A Journal from an Ehlers
Danlos Syndrome Sufferer

Chelle Calling!
(life as a zebra)

A Journal from an Ehlers
Danlos Syndrome Sufferer

Chelle Calling!
(life as a zebra)

Day 6

It's mid-morning, and I've just come downstairs. I'm sitting with a cup of coffee and my morning medication by my side: pregabalin, sertraline, omeprazole, vitamin B12, vitamin D,

I've curled up on the couch, it's a grey November day, it's raining. I clasp my cup with both hands, letting the heat work its magic against my fingers. If I haven't mentioned it before tinging and numbness in the fingers is another fabulous attribute of EDS. This often leads to struggling to grip things, or the hands just cramping up

Despite the suggested gloom, I'm sitting here, content, almost meditational, giving thanks for today.

A Journal from an Ehlers
Danlos Syndrome Sufferer

Chelle Calling!
(life as a zebra)

My granddaughter is here for the weekend, and she snuggled into bed with us earlier. Squashed herself between me and her Papa. Three of us quietly contented, Papa and Nana reading a book each and wee Teenie Bop on her phone. Moments like these are a salve to the heart and soul.

It's just contentment, a precious moment in time, like a drop of purity in a murky old world

Day 7

A Journal from an Ehlers
Danlos Syndrome Sufferer

Chelle Calling!
(life as a zebra)

My vomiting episodes over the years, pretty much had the GPs' confused. There seemed to be no physical reason for it, stomach migraines, stress related and various other ideas were mooted. they eventually concluded that, even though CVS is predominantly the realm of children, it was possible that a small percentage of adults could continue with the cycle. So that was pretty much it. Nothing could be done about it, no medical magic wand. the only proviso I was given, if the cycle went beyond 36 hours, I would need medical support, ie anti sickness medication, or an injection, or both. If that failed, then an admission to hospital would be required. I would be attached to a drip, to enable fluids, electrolytes to be replenished. Continuous vomiting takes everything from you. I also keep a box of Dioralyte or Rehidrat in the house just in case.

The most frustrating thing about CVS, is I never know when it is going to strike. Having been so stable over the last ten years, it totally shook me. It was a pretty wretched experience. I'm not under any excess stress. I'm not overly worried about anything.

A Journal from an Ehlers
Danlos Syndrome Sufferer

Chelle Calling!
(life as a zebra)

"Don't blame on the sunshine, don't blame it on the moonlight" blame it on the EDS, it sure has a lot to answer for.

Day 8

Today I had a bath. What's so special about that, I hear you ask, or even "dirty midden", how long is it, since you had a bath?

In my defence, during my CVS episode, having a bath is one of the things that seemed to help, before the cycle takes its grip.

A Journal from an Ehlers
Danlos Syndrome Sufferer

Chelle Calling!
(life as a zebra)

I've seen me at 3am, 5am, 7am, running a shallow bath, but as hot as I can reasonably bear. I lie in the dark, facecloth over my eyes, and try and let the heat of the water soothe my ravaged muscles. One advantage of having hypermobility, is the ability to use my toes to turn the hot water tap on or off. This uses the least amount of effort and movement. I then wrap myself in a towel, climb back into bed and will myself to sleep. The CVS tends to magnify all the other EDS symptoms, the exhaustion, the muscle stiffness and pain, equilibrium, overall sense of weakness.

The compulsion to bathe, runs out quickly once the vomiting pervades my system.

The first thing my husband did for me, when I came out of hospital, was to run me a hot bubble bath and helped me to get into it as well. The man is a legend, he has a lot to contend with!!!

So todays' bath was really just blissful.

It was a proper deep bath and I could just relax and let the warm water work its magic. I was able to wash myself thoroughly without pain and fear of vomiting.

Many EDS sufferers have said that a hot bath with Epsom salts does really help.

A Journal from an Ehlers
Danlos Syndrome Sufferer

Chelle Calling!
(life as a zebra)

Day 9

I'm turning into my paternal grandmother!! I've caught myself several times now, shouting "Hurrah!!" when I drop something, if something falls, or someone else drops something. My Gran used to do it all the time. I must have begun doing it about seven years ago, when my granddaughter was born, and only now realising where it stems from.

A Journal from an Ehlers
Danlos Syndrome Sufferer

Chelle Calling!
(life as a zebra)

It's difficult to do a genetic detective trail. My Gran never knew who her father was, so we can only explore as far back as her mother, which in itself has been an onerous task. My Gran would never give you a straight answer to a direct question. she would lead you a merry dancing tale, so you were never quite sure what was factual.

Similar circumstances with my paternal grandfather, he was brought up by his maternal aunt. My father doesn't know or seem to want to remember any of his family history. His sister, my aunt, will tell me a different account of events, so again limiting any factual data. Apparently, my grandfathers 'parents were some sort of travelling performers, but again that could be another interwoven, multi layered story. I have tried to research, but there is not a lot to go on. It's fair to say my father and his mother had a very cool, very distant relationship. My father was never complimentary about her and seemed to focus on her little habits, foibles and magnify them. One of them being, my Grans' obsession with cutting tags and labels from her clothing. She said they irritated her skin and that was the reasoning behind it, my father refused to grasp this.

I have to say in defence of my grandmother, I find some tags do irritate my skin and I've taken to cutting off tags and labels.

A Journal from an Ehlers
Danlos Syndrome Sufferer

Chelle Calling!
(life as a zebra)

Is it a familial weird trait or an hEDS symptom? Who knows.

A Journal from an Ehlers
Danlos Syndrome Sufferer

Chelle Calling!
(life as a zebra)

Day 10

Rolling up the hill to Slumberland (Running up that road, running up that hill, running up that building)

My first night home, first night back in my own bed, yet it finds me strangely wide awake.

Yes, I have just spent another seven nights in hospital. Damn CVS.

I didn't care that the sheets might be a bit stale. I just wanted to sleep, but each time I gently rolled up the hill (running up that road, stop it!!) I would find myself rocking at the precipice, stuck at the almost relaxed point before slumber. My mind wasn't racing. I can say

A Journal from an Ehlers
Danlos Syndrome Sufferer

Chelle Calling!
(life as a zebra)

honestly that I was feeling quite peaceful, my meds taking the edge of the aches and pains. Floating in limbo. Not quite awake, but definitely not asleep. I'd relaxed all my muscles and had done some breathing exercise, I was ready, just needed that final push, the last drop down into sleep, but it continued to evade me.

Sleep, take me, I beg of you.

And then an old nursery rhyme pops into my head

"To bed, to bed said Sleepy head

Tarry a while said Slow

Put on the pan, said Greedy Nan

We'll sup before we go!"

And now I'm chuckling to myself as I identify with all three of those characters, maybe I have a multiple personality disorder!!!

A Journal from an Ehlers
Danlos Syndrome Sufferer

Chelle Calling!
(life as a zebra)

Day 11

This evening finds me in my linen cupboard! Yes, I said in my linen cupboard. Reduced to a snivelling, useless wretch, frantically looking for an errant pillow case. It's a colour co-ordination catastrophe!!

This morning, I pulled the covers off the bed, let's get bathed and new sheets on the bed for tonight. As my bath

A Journal from an Ehlers
Danlos Syndrome Sufferer

Chelle Calling!
(life as a zebra)

was running, I went into the cupboard and selected a black duvet cover, red base sheet and black pillow cases, teamed with red for the second pillows.

I had successfully grappled with the base sheet and had got the duvet into its cover, with some assistance from the cat. She thinks it is a game, and likes to dive into the covers and roll around in them, whilst I am trying to get the bed made.

Duvet cover on, now to the pillows, unfolded the red pillowcases and discovered I only had one. Where was its partner? In the linen cupboard somewhere. So here I am stretching and pulling out duvet sets, until I realised it would be easier to actually climb into the cupboard and attempt to search in comfort. The frantic stretching and pulling had proved fruitless.

Sitting here like an overgrown garden gnome, surrounded by sheets, towels, pillowcases and finally after much searching the pillowcase finally showed up, practically the last thing in a pile of linen. How or why, I don't know, but it certainly caused great consternation!!

How these little things reduce us to anger and frustration.

A Journal from an Ehlers
Danlos Syndrome Sufferer

Chelle Calling!
(life as a zebra)

A Journal from an Ehlers
Danlos Syndrome Sufferer

Chelle Calling!
(life as a zebra)

Day 12

I really wish I could taste my coffee.

Since coming out of hospital, I'm struggling to taste it.

This is a huge disappointment to me, I love my coffee. the days that I am able to go to work, I must have two cups before I'm ready to face the world.

Hands up!! Caffeine addict!

It's probably because of the amount of medication that I'm still on, the anti-sickness tablets (metoclopramide) are to

A Journal from an Ehlers
Danlos Syndrome Sufferer

be taken three times daily for another week, reducing down to two, one, then see how I go, combined with 80mg of omeprazole, it's a wonder I can actually taste anything.

I really shouldn't grumble and just be grateful that I am eating and keeping everything where it should be.

I never really bothered about taking the omeprazole before, but I will take it religiously every day from here on in. Might take it down to a 20mg capsule though. I've also been taken off naproxen as it apparently causes stomach issues. I have an appointment in July for an endoscope, but I'm pretty sure they won't find anything, no dodgy gall bladder, stomach ulcer.

It's just another episode in the life of a zebra!!

Chelle Calling!
(life as a zebra)

Day 13

Is it just me? Or does anyone else take their clothes into the bathroom to get dressed? Invariable I am one sock short!

It is a pretty regular occurrence, the one socked wonder charging through the house!

This morning was a one sock wonder event.

Then you have to decide which foot to neglect. I mean which foot do you prefer?

If you choose the left first, is the right foot going to feel neglected and unloved or vice versa. These are the oddities that flow through my brain at times.

If your feet could talk, or had eyes, would they look at you all wounded and hurt asking why them before me.

Your poor feet are the most neglected part of your body and considering the amount of time you spend using them to stand up with, walk, climb, run, drive, etc, perhaps we should pay them a little bit more attention.

A Journal from an Ehlers
Danlos Syndrome Sufferer

Chelle Calling!
(life as a zebra)

I was recently offered a reflexology session, which was totally amazing, I thoroughly recommend trying it.

Even painting your toenails (if you can reach them), can brighten up your feet and make you smile.

A Journal from an Ehlers
Danlos Syndrome Sufferer

Chelle Calling!
(life as a zebra)

Day 14

This book seems centred around bathing!

It's Christmas Eve 2022, and I still have the childhood obsession of everything being nice and clean for Christmas, even though it is not the best of celebrations for me, I find it quite difficult and emotionally painful, but that is another story.

A Journal from an Ehlers
Danlos Syndrome Sufferer

Chelle Calling!
(life as a zebra)

My mind is cast back to massaging my mothers' legs with a nice body lotion. She was chronically unwell and the skin on her legs was always dry and flaky.

Whenever I visited, I would have my catch up chat with her whilst putting her lotion on. She loved parma violets, so I sourced a locally based company, who had a lotion with parma violet scent. I thought it would drive her crazy, but she actually loved it. I personally don't like the taste of the sweet, but do think the scent is amazing.

When I come out of my bath, I slather myself with body lotion. I know how important it is to look after your skin, soap, scrub, hydrate.

At this point for attention to fact checking and clarity, you never know who could be reading this. The woman I look upon as Mum and who I call Mum, is not my biological mother.

She lived with my father, gave him a son, my little brother, and eventually married my father.

From the very beginning she welcomed me, a moody troubled teenager, who wanted to stay with her "dad" not her mother. The biological and I were constantly in battle with each other, I had a few issues, but "Mum" was willing to take me on. I made the mistake of thinking living with "Dad" would be better. the only improvement was my

A Journal from an Ehlers
Danlos Syndrome Sufferer

Chelle Calling!
(life as a zebra)

stepmother, Mum. She was my first real friend, my confidante, my shield, everything I need a mother to be. I still miss her incredibly eight years down the line.

The biological and I haven't had any contact since 1992. I'm not even sure that she still walks the earth.

Day 15

Got up this morning, my husband was still asleep, so best to let him lie. Poor soul has the most atrocious sleep pattern.

He says that I can sleep for Scotland!! It's probably true, if I am tired nothing will prevent me falling asleep. Every

A Journal from an Ehlers
Danlos Syndrome Sufferer

Chelle Calling!
(life as a zebra)

time the weather report mentions thunder and lightning, which we rarely seem to get, I ask my husband to wake me if it happens. I love a good thunderstorm. Even as a child I loved it. I would open my bedroom window and sit there amazed. This would invariably end with my father shooing me from my perch and closing the windows and curtains.

Well I was sick again, but no panic yet, it was just the once. It was the usual though, one whole cup of coffee down the sink, but it didn't come to more than that thankfully.

A Journal from an Ehlers
Danlos Syndrome Sufferer

Chelle Calling!
(life as a zebra)

I'm still under the care of my GP, they are reducing the anti-sickness tablets. When I left hospital I was on metoclopramide three times daily and a hefty 80mg dose of omeprazole. I have to reduce down the anti-sickness week by week, before stopping altogether. I'm understandably a little bit anxious. I also understand that I cannot stay on medication long term. My sick line finishes on January the 5th and I should be returning to work, without the back up of anti-sickness meds. I have booked another appointment with my doctor; I'll ask him if I could delay work for another week.

In terms of work, I'm a dental nurse, which means I work in very close proximity with patients and my dentist. I certainly can't be vomiting in that environment.

I do have to return, ideally, I would like to take ill health retirement, but Occupational Health don't see it happening.

Technically I have two years before my NHS pension becomes available. At that point I will need to see if it is financially viable to finish working. I could always pick up a part time job at some point, if I find I'm not ready to retire.

I would love to be able to stay home with my husband. I genuinely do enjoy spending time with him.

I suppose the way to look at it, is there are less years left to work, I've got through the hard part, I have been fully

A Journal from an Ehlers
Danlos Syndrome Sufferer

employed since the age of seventeen, without any gaps in my work history.

I have been with the Health Board for twenty years, surely that has got to be worth something.

Chelle Calling!
(life as a zebra)

Day 16

I'm jumping backwards today (not literally!) Going back to the night before I was being discharged from hospital. This is my very own Nurse Rached (pronounced Rat chit) moment.

I have to admit to being absolutely furious with the way I was being treated, and in the heat of the moment I thrashed out a complaint on my iphone notes tab, fully intending to follow up on it. Now having calmed down I can ... the incident and have decided against ...

... I wrote:

Complaint: Nurses name, I had the misfortune to be transferred from ward J North on the evening of 12th

A Journal from an Ehlers
Danlos Syndrome Sufferer

Chelle Calling!
(life as a zebra)

December to ward G South at approximately 8 – 8.30pm. I had been told by staff in J North that I would be going home in the morning. so, I was quite surprised to be given a move at such a late stage. The porter came and duly moved me. I was not greeted by night staff, nor offered any orientation of my new surroundings. After waiting for around an hour I went to find some staff, they advised me they were doing a hand over and someone would come and see me. No one came near until the evening drug run at 10.30pm, I asked at that point if someone was coming to see me as I had a few questions. The curt reply was "What questions"? I asked if it was definite, I would be getting home in the morning and if someone could take my cannula out, as I was no longer being given anything by drip. "We don't have that information, who told you that? It's not on your records" I told them that both nurses and doctors in J North had said I would be discharged tomorrow, I tried to explain the distance I live from the hospital and that I had the chance of a lift home, as a relative had an appointment at this hospital at 10am and if I could leave before 11am, it would make things so much easier for me. "Well, there is nothing we can do at this time of night". Again I tried to explain the difference between being driven home or having to make my way by exceptionally patchy public transport or a very expensive taxi, they were not interested and very much "We may tell you different come the morning" By morning I could well

A Journal from an Ehlers
Danlos Syndrome Sufferer

Chelle Calling!
(life as a zebra)

have lost the opportunity of a lift home. I appreciate night staff are busy, but no one welcomed me to the ward, no one explained why I was placed on this ward and then the first interaction I receive is really abrasive and negative, almost hostile. Not impressed with G south one little bit,

Also, while I was given my evening medication, I was reading a magazine, whilst I waited for someone to bring me a drink of water to take the pills with, in comes another nurse and turns all the lights out!! all the other patients lie down like good little dollies.

At 2am the abrasive nurse came rattling through the doors with a blood pressure monitoring machine, took one patients' blood pressure, then left. she came back about ten minutes later to check the rest of our blood pressures, I asked again about having the cannula removed, I was told "not just now" At 2.30am another nurse appeared, I asked her if she could remove my cannula, which she went and asked about and returned swiftly to remove it for me.

By this point I had totally wound myself up and had given my poor husband an ear bashing over the phone. He tried his very best to placate me.

I couldn't sleep, every time I closed my eyes hot angry tears pricked my eyelids. By 6am I was in the shower, determined as soon as the shift had changed, I was out of there, I was even considering signing myself out.

A Journal from an Ehlers
Danlos Syndrome Sufferer

Chelle Calling!
(life as a zebra)

But lo and behold the day staff were lovely. they said yes you are going home; we just need the doctor to sign off, they will be with you soon. The doctor arrived and agreed I was ready for home, they were just waiting for pharmacy to dispense my medication. By now my relative had arrived and it was another waiting game. I was worried that we would run out of time, as she has a child in Primary school that would need picked up by 3pm. She was able to arrange a friend to pick her up, which was a stroke of luck.

So finally on my way home, Nurse Rached still at the forefront of my mind.

I won't go in to detail as to how she treated the other patients, except to say she was totally lacking in people skills, and sure probably have never gone into such a caring profession as nursing.

A Journal from an Ehlers
Danlos Syndrome Sufferer

Chelle Calling!
(life as a zebra)

Day 17

Todays' hot topic: EDS and the menopause. Oh Joy, I hear you groan.

Honestly though, in recent years this passage of female ageing has become less taboo, therefore people are becoming more informed and aware. In fact, the first menopause nurse/clinician in Scotland is male. My job is not to take either side on this issue, I can see both perspectives. I don't think it would do any harm for everyone to have some knowledge of what some women experience.

A Journal from an Ehlers
Danlos Syndrome Sufferer

Chelle Calling!
(life as a zebra)

Instead, I'm going to take you back to my teenage years, when I would still occasionally bunk in with my mum. Generally, on home brew nights, courtesy of my father.

She always slept with a foot out of the bed. I became obsessed with this foot. I would cover it up, she would stick it back out again. I would even wake up during the night, just to check and sure enough there would be the foot and yet again I would be compelled to cover it up. Fast forward a few years and here I am sleeping with one foot out of the bed, or my backside!! I get overwhelmingly hot in bed, so much so that the sweat causes my body to stick to the sheets. I'm not looking forward to the hot summer nights. Not only that hot flushes erupt at any given moment, they are not shy about putting in an appearance, anytime, anyplace, anywhere (who remembers the Martini advert).

So far I am coping, they only last for several minutes. My husband has become accustomed to me stripping off layers of clothing.

It can be a bit embarrassing when at work, as my job entails close contact with others. I have to wear PPE (Personal Protective Equipament) which makes you hot and uncomfortable anyway, combine that with a hot flush, it's not pleasant at all.

A Journal from an Ehlers
Danlos Syndrome Sufferer

There has been some evidence that suggests being menopausal can agitate EDS symptoms, probably a hormonal thing. So far, I've only had the hot flushes to contend with.

I wouldn't know if my forgetfulness is worse as I experience brain fog and confusion anyway.

Chelle Calling!
(life as a zebra)

Day 18

Today is the first day I have actually felt like myself.

I must admit I was anxious about an early start. I have a GP appointment at 10.30am. That's not early I hear you say. It is when you are feeling nauseous or actually vomiting.

Mornings can be a trial and it can take me a while to get organised. I can live with the EDS joint pain, even deal with the brain fog, but being nauseous all day is just soul destroying

I'm even more delighted to drink my morning coffee and not have to say goodbye to it on the way back up again.

My 7-year-old granddaughter has been staying with us this week, so that has lifted my mood and made me determined to try and rise above the nausea.

She usually spends every second weekend with us. I'm typically in agony by the time she goes home. It's my own fault, I sit on the floor with her, knowing full well I'll struggle. We build jigsaws, we draw, play cards, have mad tickling sessions, the normal things that grandparents do with grandchildren.

A Journal from an Ehlers
Danlos Syndrome Sufferer

Chelle Calling!
(life as a zebra)

We happened to be playing Hangman. Now remember it's a 7-year-old we are working with. Despite her incredible vocabulary, her spelling isn't fully developed yet. I thought it would be best to stick to subjects like, colours, animals, nature, to give her as much advantage as I could.

Then out of the blue she asks me, "Nana, how do you spell testicle?" Trying my best to conceal my shock and amusement, I asked her why she wanted to know. She came back with "It's part of your body", I replied, "Yes darling I know that" Trying to deflect now I asked her to play her word. Secretly dreading what I would be attempting to guess. On the page was a three-letter clue. Still distracted by the word testicle and desperately concealing my laughter, I could not think what her word was.

Turns out the word was eye!!! Absolutely nothing to do with testicles or genitalia, thankfully.

Thought we were going to have a "birds and the bees" moment there, phew!!

She is the most hilarious little character, and totally adorable with it.

A Journal from an Ehlers
Danlos Syndrome Sufferer

Chelle Calling!
(life as a zebra)

Day 19

Does anyone else wake up with random song lyrics in their brain?

Not sure if this is an EDS thing, more likely a Chelle thing! I have quite a few of those, foibles a plenty!!, just ask my husband.

This mornings' lyric: "When I wake up, in my make up", I can't remember the title of the song

It gets worse, on my way round to the local shop, that line was followed by "Tra la lally, here down in the valley" which I know is Tolkien, it's from a chapter in The Hobbit. Why and how these two snippets ended up linked is anybody's' guess. My brain throughs out some random shit, honestly. Oh well at least it keeps me amused.

A Journal from an Ehlers
Danlos Syndrome Sufferer

Chelle Calling!
(life as a zebra)

Apparently, apart from anxiety and EDS I'm a normal functioning adult.

And the first lyric is by Hole (Courtney Love) and it's called Celebrity skin, it would be rude of me to leave you guessing as well.

Day 20

A Journal from an Ehlers
Danlos Syndrome Sufferer

Chelle Calling!
(life as a zebra)

I would like to begin todays' entry by telling you a bit more about me.

I live on Argylls' Secret Coast, not that it is such a secret these days. We are located 25 miles from the nearest town, and a good percentage of that journey is single track roads.

Unfortunately for me, I also have travel related anxiety, which means I am a nervous driver. Unfamiliar routes are out for me, it takes me all of my time to complete those that are familiar. Some days I manage quite well, other days, the anxiety and panic win. It's a double-edged sword, in part it is a good thing to push and challenge yourself, but in another way, I want to avoid it as much as possible. I've already told you that I live 25 miles from the nearest town, I also work there. Three days a week I travel up and down this route and no two days are the same.

For ten years now I have been married to the most amazingly patient man. A right good Ayrshire lad through and through. He is loving, kind, brutally honest and ridiculously funny. His one liners are legendary, he is so quick on the uptake.

I fell in love with him when I was 14, he was 16. I had to wait 28 years to fulfil my dream. We have both made some

A Journal from an Ehlers
Danlos Syndrome Sufferer

Chelle Calling!
(life as a zebra)

incredibly disastrous and irrational decisions over those years. But we are finally together and still totally loved up.

We both enjoy live music. We book ourselves a gig, then stay overnight. so, it's really like a mini break. Some people wonder why we don't go away on holiday, but we can spend the same amount on several gigs, that people spend on a fortnight in the sun. We have seen The Stranglers (many times), Psychedelic Furs, B52s, Pixies, Marc Almond, Billy Idol, Pil, The Damned, Sisters of Mercy, Grant Lee Phillips, to name a few.

I'm lucky enough to have seen Prince twice, he will always be my idol (May U live 2 see the dawn)

We spend a lot of time with our granddaughter. She stays with us every second weekend and has done this from being 3 months old. She is my world, my joy, my heart. I thought I was lucky to finally get my man, but she is the icing on the cake.

I write poetry, I did write as a moody teenager, and recently got back into it when I lost Mum, it seemed to help, the act of writing it all down, somehow cathartic.

I like walking, though these days it is more difficult. I tire quickly and my joints protest in unison.

A Journal from an Ehlers
Danlos Syndrome Sufferer

Chelle Calling!
(life as a zebra)

I love gardening. I've never grown up; I still love grubbing around in the dirt, giving it the title gardening makes it look as though I know what I'm doing.

My mind is creative, but it doesn't always transfer in reality. I have concepts and ideas but haven't the skills to realise them.

I'm also a bookworm and always have been. Concentration can be a problem, but I persevere, as I love it too much to give it up. The book beside my bed at the moment is an Ian Rankin one.

I love horror movies and strangely Westerns, I think it is the huge vistas, and the fabulous music that draws me in.

I love to dance, always have. I suffer for it the next day though. My husband also likes dancing, he is a good dancer. Most children baulk at the idea of their parents dancing, but the last wedding we went to with our daughter, she said she loved to see us on the dancefloor. She jokingly calls it the "Pulp fiction" moment.

A Journal from an Ehlers
Danlos Syndrome Sufferer

Chelle Calling!
(life as a zebra)

A Journal from an Ehlers
Danlos Syndrome Sufferer

Chelle Calling!
(life as a zebra)

Day 21

The past few weeks I have been on a phased return to work. today was completion of my first full week. I currently work 30 hours, Monday through to Thursday.

I have to say I'm absolutely shattered. I finish work at 4.30, around 3pm I felt as though my feet were swollen and uncomfortably warm, my knees felt like leaden weights, my hips and lower back were joining the growing chorus of pain in my body. Home time couldn't come quickly enough. I was really glad that on a Thursday I cover a clinic around a mile from my home, so didn't need to worry about driving home.

I have previously mentioned being an anxious driver, but I haven't explained the pain I'm in when I drive. The pain levels I experience while driving are intense. I can manage fifteen minutes of driving before pains in my neck,

A Journal from an Ehlers
Danlos Syndrome Sufferer

Chelle Calling!
(life as a zebra)

shoulders, hips, knees, wrists and ankles kick in. Depressing the clutch is painful.

By thirty minutes, the pains increase, coupled with numbness in hands and fingers, causing cramping and spasms. The maximum time I can spend behind the wheel of a vehicle is now forty-five minutes to an hour, which is really pushing it. I then either have to stop and get out and try to get my frame straightened out or hope that I have reached my destination. Invariably, I struggle to get out of the car, due to the pain and stiffness I am experiencing. Reversing is also difficult, as it causes me pain to look over my shoulder, I try and rely on the mirrors as much as possible,

A Journal from an Ehlers
Danlos Syndrome Sufferer

Chelle Calling!
(life as a zebra)

Day 22

I'm discussing Vikings today, or rather one in particular. Ivar the Boneless, son of Ragnar Lothbrok.

Ivar lived around 775 – 870BC. He was a warrior who invaded large swathes of Ireland and England.

In fact the Vikings were the first Europeans to reach the shores of North America.

The reason I have chosen Ivar, is because of his alleged disability. Historians are divided as to whether he had Osteogenesis Imperfecta, which we commonly know as brittle bone disease, or wait for it, Ehlers Danlos Syndrome. It's nice to know I'm in such good company. Ivar didn't let his disability hold him back.

Vikings in general seemed to be an obstinate, determined bunch.

A Journal from an Ehlers
Danlos Syndrome Sufferer

Chelle Calling!
(life as a zebra)

The etymology of the word Viking possibly comes from Old Norse: meaning pirate, raider.

Vikings were Scandinavian warriors, and not particular to one country.

Their invasion of the Shetland Isles lasted for around 600 years.

The fire festival of "Up helly aa" (Holy day) is still celebrated to this day, with the largest celebration being held in Lerwick

Viking Poem:

Nobody is born a warrior

You choose to be one when you refuse to stay seated

You choose to be one when you refuse to back down

You choose to be one when you stand up after getting knocked down

You choose to be one, because if not you, Who?

This rings so true with me and I'm sure other EDS sufferers. Every day is a constant battle, to get up, get on and not give in. Yes, we are in pain in multiple areas of our bodies, yes, we get frustrated when we are unable to manage simple tasks, yes, it's tiresome dealing with brain

A Journal from an Ehlers
Danlos Syndrome Sufferer

Chelle Calling!
(life as a zebra)

fog and fatigue. But if you don't get back up and keep trying, no-one else is coming to help you,

I guess we all need to feel a little bit Viking sometimes.

Other more modern celebrities who have EDS include the comedian Russell Kane, the singer Sia and the singer/presenter Mylene Klass.

Chelle Calling!
(life as a zebra)

Day 23

I came across an old diary today and this is what I had written at that time:

The alarm goes off, on a work day at 6.20am. My first thought is "Noooo! It can't be morning already". As I reach out to turn the alarm off, my shoulder and elbow, register the first discomfort and stiffness of the day. This combined with the mornings I have numbness in my fingers and hands, not the best way to start a day. Even turning off a simple alarm becomes a difficult task.

I sit slowly up in bed, feeling all my muscles and joints groan in protest. I don't feel rested; I feel that I have been awake all night. My body feels as though it has been doing a workout during the night, not sleeping. Some nights I do wake up with numbness or pins and needles in my hands and arms.

A Journal from an Ehlers
Danlos Syndrome Sufferer

Chelle Calling!
(life as a zebra)

I swing my legs slowly out of bed, my hips registering, the pain. I won't put the light on, preferring to pad about in the dark. Bright light is not comfortable for me in the mornings. If a light is put on it makes me dazzled and more unbalanced.

To lift my clothes and walk from the bed to the bedroom door is an effort. I feel as though my body is still curled up, hunching over like an octogenarian. I gently edge my way along the end of the bed for navigation. This combined with lack of balance, which can involve me, either staggering about, or actively bouncing off walls and into door frames.

I reach the bathroom and drop my clothes behind the door. I then have to delicately lower myself on to the toilet, whilst my hips and knees register more pain and stiffness. I struggle to wipe myself afterwards, due to dexterity issues with my hands i.e. pain, numbness and tingling. Twisting my body causes pain in my hips, shoulders. By now I'm feeling nauseous and just generally under the weather. I can't contemplate a shower, the thought of trying to raise my legs over the bath, lifting my arms above shoulder height to wash my hair. I'm feeling disorientated anyway, so would not really be a safe thing to do. I make do with a wash down at the sink. I am consciously aware that I may not be adequately clean. It worries me, as I work in close proximity with clinicians and patients. This makes me anxious. The struggle to get dressed can take a while to achieve. I have difficulty lifting my arms above shoulder height in the mornings, so I spend lots of time half in, half out of t-shirts and jumpers. I tend to choose the easier option of loose fitting tops, which can be pulled over my head without too much of a fight. I hate having to disturb my husband and ask him for help.

Next job is to get downstairs. My hips, ankles and knees registering each step in protest. I boil the kettle for a cup of coffee, whilst my hands begin

A Journal from an Ehlers
Danlos Syndrome Sufferer

Chelle Calling!
(life as a zebra)

to cramp. I have had to replace the kettle twice in eighteen months, as due to lack of grip I have dropped it on the floor.

I can't face the thought of food. I feel nauseous and anxious.

I sit on the couch and drink my coffee, whilst trying to convince myself that I feel well enough to work, that I wouldn't really rather go back to bed and hide. Then I think of the patients I would be letting down if I didn't go. Wee Mrs Smith with stage 3 cancer, she will battle in regardless for her appointment. That bloke who's younger than me, but has had a stroke. He is in the midst of rehabilitation; his speech is still not great. He is always pleased to see me, because he thinks I can actually understand what he is trying to convey. If these people can manage it, then why can't I?

After I finish my coffee and taking my medication, for pain and anxiety, which I now have on an alarm to remind me, I'm good at forgetting. Then it's one final visit upstairs in case I need the toilet. I am prone to accidents, so try another seat on the toilet before I go anywhere. This however is not always successful. I brush my teeth, which causes pain in my shoulder and elbow. I have tried an electric brush, but the vibration just upsets me. I'm too sensitive in the morning.

You may ask at this point, why she doesn't take her medication before she gets out of bed. Naproxen has been prescribed twice daily. I take it before I go to work, so that any ease it may give will help me throughout the course of the working day. If I take it too early, I worry that the effects will have worn off earlier in the day and affect my ability at work. I can take paracetamol, but again I'm never very good at remembering to take medication, and once at work it can be difficult remembering due to being distracted with other work related issues. I have genuine concerns over medication as I have the added issue of CVS, I'm terrified of a

A Journal from an Ehlers
Danlos Syndrome Sufferer

Chelle Calling!
(life as a zebra)

vomiting episode, which would render me bedridden for days. Unable to do anything other than sleep, vomit on repetitive cycle.

I take the sertraline at this point as well, hoping that will cover my anxiety on my drive to work.

Then time for the main event!! Driving to work. I am already anxious. I loathe driving in the dark. I loathe driving period. I have well documented travel anxiety. My work place Occupational Health Team has put a travel caveat in place. That were possible I should drive in daylight hours and reduce the necessity to cover other clinics. I become even more anxious when it is dark, I struggle to orientate and have diminished vision when dealing with oncoming vehicles and the head light glare. I also struggle with vehicles headlamps, appearing directly behind me. I need to pull over, where I can and let the vehicles past. My familiar routes can be filled with so much anxiety and nausea, that I would not contemplate taking an unfamiliar route in the car. If ever necessitated my husband comes with me by way of public transport. He gives me the social support to engage in this activity. Left to my own devices I would struggle to get anywhere that is not familiar to me. I have been lost before and the abject terror was debilitating.

The pain levels I experience while driving are intense. I can manage fifteen minutes of driving before pains in my neck, shoulders, hips, knees and ankles kick in. To depress the clutch is uncomfortable.

By thirty minutes, the pains increase, coupled with numbness in hands and fingers, causing cramping and spasms. The maximum time I can spend behind the wheel of a vehicle is now forty five minutes. I then either have to stop and get out and try to get my frame straightened out, or hope that I have reached my destination. Invariably, I struggle to get out of the car, due to the pain and stiffness I am experiencing. Reversing is also difficult, as it causes me pain to look over my shoulder, I try and use

A Journal from an Ehlers
Danlos Syndrome Sufferer

Chelle Calling!
(life as a zebra)

the mirrors as much as possible, but it is still prudent to check visually whilst manoeuvring.

At work I try and mask how bad I am feeling. My hands don't always co-operate as they should, so passing instruments and holding suction devices and light cure devices can be tricky. The clinicians I work with are aware that I have dexterity and balance issues, they compensate where they can. This is not always feasible. Luckily I work with the Public Dental Sector, so the time we have for appointments tends to be longer than expected by a High Street Practice. I know full well, that I would not be rapid or competent enough to work in a busy practice.

I realise that not much has changed, and probably written the same words in this book already, most likely in verbatim.

It is really deflating to realise that I have not moved on, if anything my symptoms are worse, particularly with CVS rearing its ugly head again.

Today I feel as though I would benefit from being put on a rack and stretched!! Yes, it is a medieval form of torture, but just now if it would help alleviate the pain in my joints and muscles, I would happily volunteer for it.

A Journal from an Ehlers
Danlos Syndrome Sufferer

Chelle Calling!
(life as a zebra)

Day 24

My diagnosis of Ehler Danlos Syndrome was just last Summer, my GP had some new literature regarding EDS and I happened to be in seeing him about a different health matter, when we got on to the discussion of EDS.

I had previously been told by another practice that I had fibromyalgia. I had been going to the practice more local

A Journal from an Ehlers
Danlos Syndrome Sufferer

Chelle Calling!
(life as a zebra)

to my home. We moved to the Kyles of Bute almost 8 years ago, so thought it would be a good idea to register with the practice in that area. At that point I was attending appointments and discussing the amount of pain I was enduring and how widespread it seemed to be. I got the distinct impression that they didn't believe me. so I started researching by myself. One day I happened across an article about fibromyalgia and it seemed to be ticking several boxes for me.

I booked an appointment with my then GP to discuss the possibility, and I was faced with a very hostile "What is it you want me to do"? I thought to myself well you are the one with the medical degree. It gets worse, I was due a cervical smear test and booked in for it, only to discover it was the GPs' colleague that would be dealing with me.

This is where another wonderful EDS trait comes in. It is feasible for EDS sufferers to have uterine and, or rectal prolapses. In short she struggled to place the speculum, fiddled about for about 15 minutes, then said she may have to use a larger one!! She rooted about a bit more, before deciding she would ask the practice nurse to assist her, and if I would return at 1pm to try again.

So, at 1pm, I duly arrived, driving my car into the car park, about to turn the steering wheel towards a space, when BANG, !!!! The GP in her big Mitsubishi Jeep, reverses into the side of my little, tiny Clio. She then had the cheek

A Journal from an Ehlers
Danlos Syndrome Sufferer

Chelle Calling!
(life as a zebra)

to get out and say "what's going on here?" "Em, you've just crashed into to me, that's what's happened here". I still had to go back into the clinic with her and have my smear test done, I think I was just too shocked and dumbly went ahead with it.

Ram raided three times in one day!!

The next morning my neck and shoulders and right elbow were horrendously painful. I had contacted the insurance company and my little car was a complete write off. I explained the incident and they suggested claiming for personal injury, as well as giving me money to the value of my car, I think around £900 from memory. I was also able to use a courtesy car whilst the claim went through.

This incident did nothing to alleviate the pain I suffer daily, if anything it made it so much worse. Whiplash style injuries. It also shattered the little confidence I had built up as a driver. I had to start all over again.

At one point I could not even go near the driver side of a car, without anxiety and panic. I'll never enjoy driving, but I had managed to build a reasonable amount of trust with myself. That was blown right out of the water, and I had to go through the rigmarole of training myself to be less anxious behind the wheel, when all I really wanted to do was hide myself away and not take responsibility of driving a car. Which has no place in my lifestyle and the

A Journal from an Ehlers
Danlos Syndrome Sufferer

Chelle Calling!
(life as a zebra)

area that I live. Public transport is a bare minimum, and no bus gets me into town in time for work, plus the bus back out is an hour and a half after I finish work. Great in the Summer, exceptionally challenging in Winter, who wants to hang around a town that has nowhere open at that time in the evening.

A Journal from an Ehlers
Danlos Syndrome Sufferer

Chelle Calling!
(life as a zebra)

Day 25

Here we have it another humiliating episode. It was a beautiful Spring morning, so we decided to meander down to Largs for a few hours, for a browse around the shops.

Largs always amazes me, it is always a bustling little town, very popular with tourists. I wonder what it is about the town, compared to other coastal towns on the West Coast. Largs and Oban to a large extent have never stopped being perennial favourites. Whereas, Dunoon, Saltcoats have fallen by the wayside. In Saltcoats defence, it does have a busy Main Street, with a wide variety of shops to choose from. It also has some lovely cafes; you can get a decent

A Journal from an Ehlers
Danlos Syndrome Sufferer

Chelle Calling!
(life as a zebra)

lunch and a good coffee for a reasonable price. Saltcoats also has a market twice a week, with an exceptional butcher stall.

However, back to Largs. We parked the car and began wandering through the shops. I must have been oblivious to the fact that I had started jiggling my right hip and leg, as my husband passed comment that I needed the toilet. Still, me being me I thought it will be all right, lets concentrate on finishing with the shops and then I'll find a toilet.

We had gone into a toy shop, looking for super-hero figures for our granddaughter, when I realised that I would not be able to hold on after all, and told my husband I would run round to Morrisons and use the toilet there, I would see him back at the car.

I quickly hightailed it along the road to the supermarket and had got halfway across the car park when the inevitable happened. Whoosh! my bladder decided to empty itself completely, right through my jeans, knickers, down into my socks.

Mortally embarrassed I ran back to the car. I told my husband what had happened, and he was concerned as to what I was going to do, I couldn't get in the drivers' seat

A Journal from an Ehlers
Danlos Syndrome Sufferer

Chelle Calling!
(life as a zebra)

with my soaking wet clothes. Fortunately, I had bought a pair of jeans in one of the shops, so I hastily got them out of the boot and was going to climb into the car to change.

My husband told me to go back to the supermarket toilet and change, I was so anxious and embarrassed I couldn't even think to do that. I then had to spend the rest of the day "commando "not very pleasant I can tell you. My husbands' thoughts are I should wear skirts more often, at least that way it would avoid flooding myself.

The sad thing is that it isn't the first time this has happened to me. My uterine muscles just don't have the capability of holding off for a great length of time.

If I need the toilet, then I need to go, fairly quickly, why I still attempt to hold off is ridiculous, stupid pride probably.

A Journal from an Ehlers
Danlos Syndrome Sufferer

Chelle Calling!
(life as a zebra)

A Journal from an Ehlers
Danlos Syndrome Sufferer

Chelle Calling!
(life as a zebra)

Day 26

Today I'm focussing on work/life balance. for most of my adult life I have been employed full time hours, Over the last fifteen years it has been increasingly difficult for me to maintain full employment and having energy left for my life outside of work,

I have reduced down to thirty hours, which means I have a Friday to myself. It gives me an extra day to recuperate before, yet another working week commences. It also means I can spend more time with my husband, or potter about the garden if the weather is reasonable.

Modern life now expects both husband and wife to be out working, gone are the days when mothers stayed home for

A Journal from an Ehlers
Danlos Syndrome Sufferer

Chelle Calling!
(life as a zebra)

the first five years with the children, then went back to work part time.

Prior to the outbreak of World War 2, the "norm", was that the man was the breadwinner and the women stayed home and kept house. It was not unusual for a woman to give up her job or be expected to give up her job at the point of marriage.

With the majority of able-bodied men being recruited into the forces, a labour shortage was experienced. Women were called into factories, agriculture and various other aspects of employment to shore up the country.

When the men returned after the war, females were not so keen to return to being the little kept woman, and society began to change.

Bankers capitalised on this, offering mortgages based on two wages. Landlords quickly followed suit.

Nowadays, both adults in the household work, pay a mortgage, have vehicles on hire purchase, expect their two weeks in the sun as a matter of right. A holiday is no longer seen as a luxury. The rise of credit cards and the possibility of having pretty much whatever you want on hire purchase agreements.

For me, I own my car, it isn't a new car, it's around thirteen years old, but it does what I need it to do. I'm proud that I am not paying out every month.

A Journal from an Ehlers
Danlos Syndrome Sufferer

Chelle Calling!
(life as a zebra)

I no longer own a credit card, learnt the lesson the hard way, If my husband and I need or want something, we are happy to save up for it. I'm a great believer if you don't have the cash in your hand to pay for it, then walk away. If you feel that it is something that you must have, then save up for it,

In the past I've had to sell a car in order to pay a massive electricity bill. I now have a prepayment meter.

My husband is long term sick, so unable to work. I would dearly love to drop another day, but we are already on the cusp of where we need to be financially. My wage covers the rent, council tax, car costs, general bills and outlays.

We both chip in on food shopping. If we do have a treat like a night away, I pay the hotel and he covers food and anything else we need. It's a successful system for us.

In an ideal world I would not be working, the daily aches, pains and other complications that come with EDS, would be so less challenging if I was Mistress of my own routine. Ultimately, it's all about finance and keeping the wolf from the door.

I'm hoping that in two years' time, (when I'm 55) that my NHS pension offers a decent lump sum, and I could maybe think about retiring.

A Journal from an Ehlers
Danlos Syndrome Sufferer

Chelle Calling!
(life as a zebra)

My days of bending over backward to help my workplace are over. I used to agree to work extra hours, come in on my days off, start early, finish late and never complain. It gets you absolutely nowhere, no extra thanks, no appreciation, just more strain on an already aching body. I was conditioned to be that way, learned behaviours, which I am slowly trying to unpick and retrain myself. I'm not saying that I don't care, I do, I just need to start putting myself first, not continuing to be a slave to the grind.

Roll on retirement!! I know a lot of people who don't want to retire and wouldn't know what to do without their job, I can't see me having that problem.

I happened to be listening to the radio and they were discussing The French coming out on strike, as their government want to increase the retiral age from 62 to 64. 62 is a perfect age to finish working life, perhaps the UK should look at it, instead of pushing us towards a mid 70 retirement date. You have got to love the French for their sheer militarism. In this country we are too willing to roll over and accept the capitalist Tory nonsense.

Finding a happy work/life balance is the dream.

A Journal from an Ehlers
Danlos Syndrome Sufferer

Chelle Calling!
(life as a zebra)

Day 27

A Journal from an Ehlers
Danlos Syndrome Sufferer

Chelle Calling!
(life as a zebra)

I have realised as I've gone on with this book, that I am revisiting parts of my past with a bit more understanding. For example, I have always been concerned about my "scraggly" neck, as I call it. It worried me that I always had an old looking neck, if that makes any sense. It has always looked wrinkled and stretchy, I know understand that this is a visible symptom of EDS. Don't get me wrong it isn't wobbling about like a turkey neck, but I have always felt very conscious of it.

The other thing I am finally realising is why I have trouble using a paint brush.

From a very young age, my hands would cramp and become very painful. I used to own a cottage that had stone outhouses. I had fashioned tongue and groove doors for them, and aimed to coat them in creosote. I had no sooner started with the brush, when my hands started to react, the fingers themselves were cramping and I found it increasingly difficult to hold the brush. I couldn't understand it, and every year when the time came to paint the doors, I would have to go through the suffering just to complete the job.

Only now, can I look back and say yes EDS strikes again.

A Journal from an Ehlers
Danlos Syndrome Sufferer

Chelle Calling!
(life as a zebra)

I used to really enjoy baking, but the whipping and beating involved causes me too much pain, I can't even grate a bit of cheese without experiencing immense pain.

A Journal from an Ehlers
Danlos Syndrome Sufferer

Chelle Calling!
(life as a zebra)

Day 28

In a rare impulsive moment I booked us two nights away in Campbeltown. My husband has never been, and I have no recollection, I may have visited as a child, but don't actively have a memory of it.

My initial thought to cut down on the driving was to take the ferry from Portavadie (15 minutes from my door) to West Loch Tarbert, which would leave me around an hour of driving, which \i thought fair enough, I'm being upbeat I can do this.

But true to Caledonian MacBrayne form, the ferry wasn't sailing. We were now facing a three-hour journey on unfamiliar roads. I have been as far as Kennacraig in a car, as a passenger many times, but haven't driven it myself until now. The only way we could manage was to factor in stops along the way.

First stop Inverary, grab a coffee and stretch the bones, then on to Lochgilphead, fuel up the car and have another stretch, before ploughing on to Campbeltown. Luckily the roads were fairly quiet, another couple of weeks an it will be tourist season. So that was an added bonus.

A Journal from an Ehlers
Danlos Syndrome Sufferer

Chelle Calling!
(life as a zebra)

By the time we arrived in Campbeltown I was in agony from top to bottom.

The room we were given at the hotel had the most amazing mattress, which was just as well, I was really pretty crippled.

Still it was nice to have a couple of nights away and the weather held for us as well. Campbeltown itself has a lovely feel to it and the people are friendly. I'm sure it is a bustling wee place during tourist season. The Kintyre 66 will have many motoring fans. For me I was just delighted that I had managed the drive, with tremendous support from my husband. I would never have even contemplated such an expedition without him, my anxiety would have taken over.

On route home we arrived in Tarbert, hoping that the ferry may be back in action. Alas, a limited service, next sailing 16.30pm. It was only 10.30am at this point. We had something to eat in one of the little cafes there, before getting back underway. Again, the traffic was light, so no major hassles, or being stuck in a convoy of wood lorries and tankers, which is quite normal for that route, particularly from Inverary down to the Cairndow road end.

We may not have done much while we were away, but I remain proud of my achievement.

A Journal from an Ehlers
Danlos Syndrome Sufferer

Chelle Calling!
(life as a zebra)

We were also home in time for my husband to watch his beloved Rangers game.

Day 29

A Journal from an Ehlers Danlos Syndrome Sufferer

Chelle Calling!
(life as a zebra)

I must admit to spending most of this day in a vegetative state. Glad to be back home, but tired and sore, any chores about the house down to a bare minimum. My husband was also feeling below par, so most of the day was spent watching films and catching up on Question Time and Debate Night. We have them on series link recording.

I must confess to watching Celtic beat St Mirren 5 – 1, the rivalry in our house is of a friendly nature. I cannot understand those that use football as a divisive tool. Football is a game, and should be treated as such, there is no room for political, religious or racist beliefs designed to influence which team you support.

I'm of the opinion each to their own, as long as you don't bother me with it, don't put your influences on me. The one good thing I can say about my parents, when it came to religion, we were left to make up our own minds, we were encouraged to ask questions. My paternal Grandpa was a very devout Irish Catholic (I never knew my dads' natural father; this was the only man I knew as my grandparent). He worked hard, he played hard. He would finish work on a Saturday morning, straight in to the working man's club in Wishaw. The man could drink like a fish!! He would then collect a fish supper for my Gran, before putting on his "Rebel" songs, which he would expect you to join in with. If you didn't know the words,

A Journal from an Ehlers
Danlos Syndrome Sufferer

then you best mime them, otherwise the temper would flare.

My Mum (step mother) dallied with the Jehovah Witness teachings off and on throughout her life, so I certainly have a very skewed concept of religion. Don't get me wrong for those who do have that commitment of faith, I respect them for it, but it isn't for me at all.

Chelle Calling!
(life as a zebra)

Day 30

Well, Dear reader, there you pretty much have it, my life as a zebra.

Majority of days, you get up, plaster the smile on your face and get on with it.

If you give in at all, EDS will steal more from you.

I understand that I'm not as fit as I used to be, when I was younger, I found ways to compensate. In truth, it's getting harder to compensate. I don't have the same amount of strength anymore.

I was once, a morning person, up with the lark, getting some house hold chores done before I went to work and also getting involved with things after work, but the energy

A Journal from an Ehlers
Danlos Syndrome Sufferer

Chelle Calling!
(life as a zebra)

has sapped, I'm quite happy to see my couch after a day at work.

It may not be the most exciting of existences, but I like my life, I'm comfortable with where I am at. I love my husband, feel overwhelming love in return from him. Completely adore my girls. Never happier than when I'm pottering about my garden, or cosied up in bed with a good book and of course my coffee!!

A Journal from an Ehlers
Danlos Syndrome Sufferer

Printed in Dunstable, United Kingdom